MW00653877

SINGLE FAMILY
VALUES

TAQUILLA R. CLARK

This publication contains the opinions and ideas of its author. It is intended to provide helpful and informative material on the subjects addressed in the publication. The author and publisher specifically disclaim all responsibility for any liability, loss, or risk, personal or otherwise, which is incurred as a consequence, directly or indirectly, of the use and application of any of the contents of this book.

WRITERS REPUBLIC L.L.C.
515 Summit Ave. Unit R1
Union City, NJ 07087, USA

Website: *www.writersrepublic.com*
Hotline: *1-877-656-6838*
Email: *info@writersrepublic.com*

Ordering Information:
Quantity sales. Special discounts are available on quantity purchases by corporations, associations, and others. For details, contact the publisher at the address above.

Library of Congress Control Number:		2021922103
ISBN-13:	978-1-64620-872-2	[Paperback Edition]
	978-1-64620-873-9	[Digital Edition]

Rev. date: 11/03/2021

CONTENTS

———

DEDICATION

I dedicate this book to a wonderful Single Mother who was perfectly imperfect, a hero to her three sons, and an inspiration to me, my sister VALENCIA L. CLARK 04-30-2010 R. I. P.

INTRODUCTION

Thank you for your purchase, I want you to begin by gracefully saying, this is not a way of life I will encourage, and if you're in this place, I want to help you make the best of every moment. I'm excited for you because you want better for yourself & your family, you want to produce, progress, and be the best you can be, not just for yourself but for your family. The reason behind this book being written, Being a single parent has its ups, and without a shadow of doubt, it has its downs. Sometimes when it rains in your life, it's more than just a few showers, feels like a rainstorm. Most of all I wanted to make a difference in someone's life, hopefully starting with you. I am a single mother of three and have studied early childhood education for 15 years plus, and I'm currently in the process of manifesting my own facility **Kommunity Insight Discovery Zone Inc.** Which I have procrastinated for the last 10 years because of doubt, but no more. This book is the 1st step of me stepping out on faith to reach my goals, Therefore I thank you for your support along this journey. Experience qualifies me as a Mother and Teacher. I'm aware this book may not benefit every set of hands, but I want to touch and agree with you, that you & your family lives will begin to overflow with great success and fun with this book of tips, encouragement, and experiences in my life. I would like to thank God almighty and say that I'm extremely grateful for my family who has been the village in my children's lives. My mother who I can never re-pay for her endless love, compassion, and a caring heart. My daughter's God Mother Teresa, a strong single mother in my circle, my father who supported me when I needed him, my sister crystal who inspired me to write this book who always have an opened ear to listen, My oldest sister Iris, who has always taught me how to protect myself because I'm a single Mother, the extra precautions I have to take. This book is based on the experiences I have lived, live, and look forward to living. And a lot learned along this journey thus far.

*There are some stop and think notes along the way. Opportunity to write your thoughts down.

CHAPTER 1

BEING A SINGLE PARENT

Being a single parent is no easy task alone, and you have to remember no one does it to perfection. There are different styles and techniques to raising kids, you play two roles but you only get one roll packed down, and that's knowing how to be the Mother, or in some cases the Farther, and we do the best we know-how. For myself, this is not the fairytale nor the future I envision for myself. But let me first say this, I do not regret a moment of it, there are challenges and I'm sure you can relate, and it has made me the woman I am today

- Having one (child) or children = more than one personality besides your own = dealing accordingly to the individual needs

- You choose your battles carefully either you be the good guy or the bad guy

- Mean what you say & say what you mean, there is no one else to follow up or be consistent with (punishment) or re-enforce rules when you forget.

- You have a handle on being there for your kids, but then that means the job performance lack or you have a handle on the job than the kids lack the attention needed

- Single parent life consist of weekends with kids most of the time,

Now don't feel bad, it comes with the territory of being a Single Parent and we learn along the way, it's a very critical situation when the other half is not there for support emotionally, mentally, physically, or financially.

Stop and Think

What are your challenges of being a single parent?

_____

_____

_____

_____

_____

As parents, we must allow our children to have a voice to communicate with us. Assure them they will not get into any trouble, and you are there to listen with no interruptions or judgment. Our kids may not always have someone else to express how they may feel about a form of discipline, decisions, or changes inside and outside the household. Respectfully and humbly give your child a time for one on one, or arrange family dinner, a family night of fun and be open mentally emotionally with open ears.

Choosing your battles is not always easy. But you have to decide, according to the situation, you have to stick to it, if you're going to be the good guy and show mercy this time you can't go back and punish for the same situation moments later. Now if you decide to be the bad guy you can't let up, see the punishment through, otherwise, the child will notice an inconsistent pattern and not take you seriously, MEAN WHAT YOU SAY & SAY WHAT YOU MEAN.

Me time and adult time with friends are mandatory. Eventually, Single Parent life becomes overwhelming to you, and when this happens you become overwhelming to everyone else around you. And this only causes tension and soon pushes you to a breaking point, and that tension does not only rest on you, but it rests on your family as well, affecting their performance and communication at home and outside the home.

ME TIME:

Below are some tips that can help to relieve stress and tension in your life, allow one or more to be your outlet because life goes on with or without you.

OUTLET= LET IT OUT and LET IT GO

- Exercise
- Yoga
- A night out with friends or sibling
- Catch a movie (comedy)
- Go to a nearby cafe, or park to catch up on a good book
- Choose an activity outside the box, and out of your element
- Go out to the beach to meditate

Chapter 2

WHAT ARE FAMILY VALUES

FAMILY VALUES are who and what we make time to build and nurture. Traditions, legacy, dedication, blending different personalities and points of view on life, with respect. Able to value and accept each person for who they are and where they are with no judgment, knowing and trusting, if I'm not accepted, appreciated, or loved anywhere else in this world, I can look to my family with flaws and all. FAMILY VALUES take work, but the rewards are so much greater, the trust and growth in relationships between a mother and her kids/father and his kids, sister and brother makes it all worth it. Knowing it comes in different colors, shapes, and sizes. Proud of the fact Family Values can still be built even if a father or mother is absent, don't stop living, you can still enjoy life together, so I say value and cherish what we put into our families. And when someone comes along, such as companionship, they add value to your family, not bringing value because the value has already been established.

You can still teach your child family values, have family outings and go on family trips, etc... You may not be able to do it as often as a family with two parents financially, but it can be done.

Family night does not always consist of spending money. It can be as simple as sitting playing board games or outdoor games, TIME is something we can't get back, but we can always begin again,

Why is family important to you?

_____

_____

_____

_____

_____

_____

How do you OR how will you build values with your family?

_____

_____

_____

_____

_____

_____

We don't always have time but we can always make time, just a matter of doing so, a quote I love, quality over quantity, what does that person bring to the table, we seek to build, not tear each other down.

QUANTITY: We meet very often, but only sit and gossip with that person, and there's no value in your conversation, no encouragement, no inspiration, negativity, complaints.

QUALITY: I see you rarely, but when you talk with that person, they make you think, you are motivated, you are excited about a movement, a change within your mindset, positive and happy thoughts.

It's ok to question what someone brings into your life because you don't want anyone to destroy what you've taken time to build. Be aware they either come to give and receive or only come to receive. We all know when you're the one constantly giving and never receiving eventually you have no more to give. And once the person has taken all they can take, there's no other interest at that point in the relationship.

Know your value and know the value you have placed within your family, I'm not only referring to companionship, we have family and friends that we have to be mindful of, they sometimes have different values in their families and yours may be different.

Be sure that you agree upon the same things because you are exposing your family to a different environment, and you want to be sure your child know and hold to their values taught, having respect for themselves, and for me as their guardian, I know times are different now, but there are some things I wanted to hold on to when raising my kids, teach them to respect themselves and you will not have to worry about them disrespecting you or others, not to say they will not have experiences, but they know they have choices, we hear it all the time " IF YOU DON'T STAND FOR SOMETHING, YOU WILL FALL FOR ANYTHING" I was taught respect and I also was taught Boundaries, if I took a chance on something, understanding there is a cause and effect, what may seem to be ok with someone else may not be ok with you, simply because your values are different, your standards are different, and there's nothing wrong with that, and I'm not saying don't leave your kids with family, I'm saying don't sit back and assume they know the values you teach.

BUILDING A RELATIONSHIP
WITH YOUR KID/KIDS

- Take Time To Relate => Communicate => Build Family Values

Dedicating time is not always accessible that's why it's called dedication; it does not just present itself. Set aside time for yourself, this is very important because for you to have time for anyone else. I've personally learned I must first have time for myself; my methods are prayer and meditation, etc.

I try to have (quiet time) in a quiet place in the morning before anyone else rises, it allows me to center myself, I have to attend to myself 1st. Now I can focus on everyone else who needs me in my circle, this will remind you to not forget about yourself.

Individual needs are met better between you and your child. This is guaranteed with toddlers, adolescent, teenagers, and even relationships with adults,

These are methods used to dedicate time to your kids, and you don't always have to ask what they want to do because your pockets are not always sufficient enough for what they want to do. There are some good fun free activities to do with your kids even at home and remember kids don't expect much they just want your time more than anything else.

- The Beach is always a fun activity and it will exhaust all energy your child may have, just remember to take a cooler with snacks
- Get your local newspaper to find fun family events in town or downtown
- Get a recipe from your local food store to find items and cook together, this is a good and fun way to also introduce new foods to your family
- Go on a nice bike ride together
- Take a trip to the library/ join activities at your local library, Saturdays are the best days sometimes

Don't be afraid to know what your kids think of you, here's a fun list of questions to ask your kids during moments of communication, do not get offended or angry with your kids, and without prompting or any guidance, ask these questions, allow them to answer on their own, freely, no interruptions with verbal, body language or facial expressions unless you're laughing.

1. What is something I say a lot?
2. What makes me happy?
3. What makes me sad?
4. How tall am i?
5. How old am I?
6. What's my favorite thing to do?
7. What makes you proud of me?
8. What's my favorite food?
9. Do you think you could live without me?
10. How do I annoy you?
11. hat is my favorite TV show?
12. When is my Birthday?

Another point I found to be very helpful, new places, such as, restaurants, parks, take different routes home, this is opportunity to see new things to open their imaginations, perhaps a different neighborhood than where they live, try new activities, I've always used Groupon to find so many different activities for my family to get into, you will not be disappointed, I remember me and my kids went on a Jet Boat Ride, the anticipation was high, everyone was dressed for the occasion, the ride was wet and wild, drove me a little crazy, everyone was soaked and wet, but their response to that event was "wow" my daughter who was scared when it all began, shouted " let's go again" so she overcame a fear through this event, which made me smile from the inside out.

I remind my kids from time to time, think outside the box, don't let your atmosphere make you so comfortable, you never dream or hope for nothing more, or bigger, to the point you're satisfied where you are, don't get comfortable saying these words "I have enough" I believe you've stopped living and experiencing at this point. Your imagination is still on the move, your dreams are as real as you make them, and another day is another opportunity to engage in something new.

This message tell your kids there is more to life than my present moment, listen to their dreams, encourage their imagination because that is the life they see for themselves, and it's up to us as parents to nurture the dreams and the very things they imagine, I strive to encourage my kids dreams, my daughter wants to be a Neonatal Nurse, so I speak of this often and do things to encourage this and she has yet to change her mind, she has been using a thestiscope since the age of seven for herself because she has asthma, therefore she's very aware of what's she's listening for within her lungs, this little bit has encouraged her to be all that she hope for, I believe in her mind she's gonna do just that because she's now fifteen and it's still all she talks about, My middle son wants to be a professional gamer and yes i support his dreams even if i didn't fully understand it, but i believe he will soar because he has the opportunity to fulfill that dream, my oldest son in college now yet and still wants to be a professional football player, and I'm grateful i have the opportunity to help them fulfill their dreams, what they envision for themselves. Some may not agree but I believe your kids tend to live a happier life doing what they love, rather a slave to obligation only to exist, but not living, when you do what you love, you love what you do, and you're less likely to grow tired of that dream that has become a reality, at least until old age. Live your best life

DATING MR. OR MRS. RIGHT

Dating is challenging enough, not to mention when you have kids it just adds more pressure to the idea of dating when you have your family to protect, there are so many things to put into perspective or so we think, honestly it's not that serious that's why it's called dating and you don't have to rush to make decisions about everything right away, relax and learn how to enjoy the moment for yourself, don't even think of going into too much detail about your kids on a first date, of course, make sure it's known you have a (kid) or kids, you really don't know who you're talking to, don't give up everything on the first date there will be more time to discuss and get to know each other further if appropriate

Some things to consider before getting serious and introducing a man to your kids, at least know the potential of the relationship, I heard a sermon from Pastor Dale Bronner titled: derailed relationships, on YouTube "what is the history of that person's decisions, who's voice do they trust because you may not be building a relationship with them but the person that has the biggest impact on their lives, he uses a method called F.A.C.E.S" you can check out the video on YouTube for more insight on this topic, but this is the biggest thing that stood out to me when considering getting to know someone and possibly introducing them to my kids, learn of them as much as you can.

F-Family Background

A- Attitude

C-Compatibility

E- Experiences that they have had

S- Skills that they bring to a relationship

Don't let anyone pressure you into a relationship because your kids don't have a Father or Mother present physically in the home, it is not the end of the world, just a different world that you have taken time to add value to and make the best of every opportunity. The only way someone comes to be a part of your family is if they have something great to add to your family structure, (VALUE) society tends to see things the way they think life should be, unfortunately, life does not always plan out the way we envision for ourselves for one or more reasons, I want to encourage you to bravely take a hand, lend a hand when needed, below are some good books you can use for guidance they helped me and I believe that will help you as well

Steve Harvey "Act like a lady thinks like a man" part 1, part 2 gives more detail and insight as everyone began to have questions about part 1, but it's so much more in-depth, and really answers the questions women have in general.

"God where is my Boaz?" This book is more so for women who need a little direction getting back out on the dating scene and what to expect, brush up on some things, deal with past issues, begin to move forward in a positive direction, be mindful of the type of energy you put out because that's what you will receive.

Don't look at being single like it's a disease or the worst thing in the world, it's actually the time to mold the best you that you want to see in you, take time to value yourself, enjoy being single creating your happiness, be realistic, also be open and honest with yourself and find out what it is, you really like to do on downtime, what type of vacations would you take, or just for fun take a class, take time to figure out what you like and dislike, learn how to just feel good about you, attraction comes from within, don't wait to live, live now, exercise your body and mind read new things, try new things broaden your surroundings and your life daily, as much as possible, commit to you, do not spend any time in regret, this makes dating and conversation easier when dating. Embrace you, love you, understand you, respect you, trust you, be nice to you, be honest with you, this way you can show and tell people how to treat you.

JOB/KIDS

This was the challenge that got me every time because I was trying to dedicate myself to my job and stay on track while I continue to provide for my family. But it was always either the job or my family will be on the back burner, with my kids it was either the issues of staying on task in school or at home with chores and homework, attending sports or more than one event at a time, never-ending. Of course, I wanted to progress and get higher positions to make more money but at what cost, what would I have to sacrifice to keep a steady income, I've passed up great opportunities and I can't say that I regret a moment I've chosen to be there for my babies,

Balancing kids and job performance. I had to learn, first of all, don't accept a job that does not work for your needs, otherwise, you will not only inconvenience your family life but you inconvenience the employer as well because you were not prepared for the position offered, the money sound good and the benefits look good, but to maintain a balance in your family life and work, you have to select something that works for everyone, there are so many things we do regularly that can make us money from baking, sewing, building, helping and assisting others at a cost, whatever it is that you do well, has an opportunity to turn out to be more than a hobby. There is a God-given gift in everyone and then there are things you've learned and gained experience from. I currently work to provide, save and fund my vision for my business, until I'm able to open and maintain stability for at least the 1st year of business.

Currently, entrepreneurship is on the rise, not everyone will find this to be the best route, being the only provider in the home, some single parents cut costs by homeschooling their kids, once they're able to run a fully functional successful business. Remember to always do what's convenient and best for you and your family but know that you have options, below are some points for potential entrepreneurship.

- Think about your hobby or hobbies

_____
_____
_____
_____
_____
_____

- What are you good at with the least amount of effort?

_____
_____
_____
_____
_____

- What are you most passionate about, makes you smile inside out?

_____
_____
_____
_____
_____

- Are you able to save, or get a loan to fund your vision? List your options.

_____

_____

_____

_____

_____

_____

- Are you willing to make the sacrifice? Really think about what the sacrifice will be.

_____

_____

_____

_____

_____

_____

Some families have the convenience of working from home, this causes you to focus on your family more and meet their needs better, speaking from experience, do your research before accepting any offers, it's always better to work with well-known companies and or word of mouth of someone who currently works from home to avoid scams, protect yourself and be mindful of financial investments you may be eager to make when deciding to work from home.

CHAPTER

6

DREAMS ON HOLD

Note: {You support everyone else dreams around you, don't forget about you and yours}

What are your hopes and dreams? What are the things you want to accomplish before you leave this world? Do you believe you can still reach those goals? Well don't let anyone tell you otherwise, please believe you can reach your goals after having kids, of course, your priorities change but your still alive therefore you still have an opportunity to reach every desire, vision, and dream you may have. If you feel like your life is over because you have kids, that means you have limited yourself and have stop living, which is not fair to you, your family, and others around you, I told myself one day if I'm not living to my fullest potential how can I push my kids to reach their goals.

Adult time should be mandatory in your life because eventually life naturally becomes overwhelming, and it doesn't have to be intentional, But it would only cause tension and soon push you to make decisions based on your emotions and not what we know to be right.

Time can be spent chasing your dreams or hobbies, but whatever you do, use your time wisely, dedicate yourself even if it's only two to three times a month you will be surprised to discover the change those small increments of me time will allow. Your dreams will come alive before your very eyes, it's not about how fast you get there, but what you do to get there, as long as you stay committed.

Below are some tips that can help to relieve stress and tension in your life, allow one or more to be your outlet because life goes on with or without you, and your dreams would have been nothing but a dream… and you deserve more.

OUTLET= LET IT OUT and LET IT GO

- Exercise

- Yoga

- Spiritual connection, meditation

- Night out with friends or sibling

- Catch a movie (comedy) preferred

- Go to a nearby cafe, or park to catch up on a good book

- Choose an activity outside the box, outside your element

- Go out to the beach and relax

- Go to a nice jazz spot for some love music

Stop and Think

What are your dreams and aspirations?

_____

_____

_____

_____

_____

_____

What kind of time could you dedicate to yourself every month? Be honest and realistic.

_____

_____

_____

_____

_____

_____

Try prioritizing your life in a way that will make more time for you to dedicate time to your dreams as well, fulfill your purpose, be better for yourself first, and then for everyone else around you, take that time for you to be all that God has created you to be.

Psalms 23:5 my cup runneth over

When I read this verse I think of it as, let me fill me up first, and then when I overflow that's me being able to help someone else because I have so much to give now.

CHAPTER

7

TAP INTO YOUR SUCCESS

To tap into success, you must change your mindset, causing you to do something you've never done before, turning you in a direction you've never thought of or simply avoided going, it's like taking the same route home every day because you're familiar with that direction, you've become accustomed to the traffic, the annoying lights taking that familiar route and you dare not chance another route because you assume all the routes are the same so it doesn't make any sense to go that way, honestly, going the same way every day is frustrating but you endure it.

Until one day you decide, today is the day I'm taking a chance. Along the new route, you see some new things and places that don't even allow you to focus on the traffic or the lights, but the fact you're getting where you're going with very little effort, and all you can ask yourself is, "why didn't I take this route sooner, what was I thinking" like most of us do, but don't get stuck thinking what I should've, could've, would've done.

Instead began to move forward forgetting what's behind, and that will encourage you to try another route eventually. I went on a trip to the Bahamas, it was my first time on the island. It was an amazing experience for me totally out of my element. I got seasick on the way to the island, but it didn't spoil my excitement. I had to just get to the destination. Just the process of doing and not questioning or hesitating was an accomplishment, what I realized at that moment, I have waste time by procrastinating bouncing back and forth with the ideas but not putting any of them into action, well times have changed and I'm looking forward to the next trip, next adventure, whatever it may be.

Stop and Think:

What was the last thing you envisioned, or thought of doing but didn't get to it right away but now you think you're ready?

_____

_____

_____

_____

_____

_____

As a result of procrastination, what is it you haven't accomplished as of yet, that you will still love to do?

_____

_____

_____

_____

_____

_____

Ask yourself, what will I do differently to transform my mindset to get the things I desire?

_____
_____
_____
_____
_____
_____

What is it that you'd like to accomplish? What and or who can you let go of to get there?

_____
_____
_____
_____
_____
_____

Once you figure out what you want to accomplish and how you're gonna get there, then you can begin to set plans and carry them out, don't expect everything to come out just as you planned it, there will be obstacles no matter what route you take, it's all in how you deal with the bumps along the way, whatever you do, don't allow it to push you back causing you not to get back up and try again, For myself I had many setbacks and even though I might have taken a while to get back up I did eventually get back up and as a result of it this book is one of my proudest moments, my set back has been about 10yrs, but I'm back up and ready to fight again, the desire doesn't die. It wasn't just because things weren't going as planned but also I was afraid of failing again, doubting that little old me can have such success, driving around in such a beautiful candy apple red Mercedes and changing people's lives as I envision so often, picturing myself singing on stage in front of millions, words of wisdom in my music, changing lives every day. Believe in you, fight for you, do it for you first, then you will see the change in everyone else around you.

NO DISTRACTIONS

I've set goals, and I can never seem to reach them, every time I get to the middle I find myself quitting, what am I doing wrong? Are you asking yourself these questions? Hopefully, this chapter helps you put things into perspective.

What do you consider distractions for yourself?

_____

_____

_____

_____

_____

_____

What goals have you set currently, but can't seem to stay focused on?

_____

_____

_____

_____

_____

_____

What do you think the problem is? And how do you plan to change it?

_____

_____

_____

_____

_____

_____

Well, the good news is that everyone gets distracted at some point, but it's what you do when those distractions come along, that's when we have to choose and desire to do what makes us feel good, but I've learned if I operate based on how I may feel about doing the work, I want to get much done, just being honest with myself.

No matter who you are, it can be hard to focus on the goals you set to complete a task especially when it's something you don't really want to do and or don't find fun to do. Unfortunately, we will allow the smallest distractions to take place so we can have an excuse to quit and or stop for now, and our mindset becomes, "oh I'll get to it tomorrow" and that turns into, "oh I'll get to it this weekend" etc. This type of thinking can derail your productivity, and cause procrastination, don't allow this to happen to you, whether it's going back to school, or you set out to find a way to generate more income for your family, have more family time, maybe you want to set a goal to eat dinner with family at least 3 nights out of the week, whatever you set out to do change your mindset to overcome distractions, set goals you can commit to, below are some tips that may help when setting REALISTIC goals.

- Set days and times you know for a fact there will be no distractions, NO mommy duties, NO work, NO classes, NO meetings, etc.

- Dedicate to a time frame to focus on the work, start with 30 minutes to an hour, anything more than that takes 10-15 minute breaks in between

- Track how you spend the time, break the task down into sections.

- Put the cell phone away.

- Train your brain to focus, start working in small increments, push to progress

- Be patient with yourself.

CHAPTER 9

I AM NOT A STATISTIC

You may be thinking "how i got to this point" married young 18 years old because of my 1st son and wanting out of that situation as a confused young woman looking for love and security, i moved on prematurely to an absent minded and confused young man, having my second child and then turn having my third child by the same absent minded and confused young man, now a single mom of 3, I knew i didn't want people to see how i felt about me and when someone stop to admire my kids, they didn't forget to remind me how young i was with three kids, so I've always set a standard for myself and my kids with God in the plan and These are words i spoke to inspire myself after having my daughter, i was feeling ashamed, hurt and mighty low, but encouraged to live my best life, work 2 jobs to get out the environment i had my kids in, the rent was cheap but my life was not what i wanted nor expected, my parents didn't raise me in that lifestyle, i knew i couldn't result to that and be ok with it, change had to happen, most of all my parents gave me God (prayer) therefore i had a fight in me that demanded more of me.

I'm not your label (baby mama)

I'm not her

Not the typical single mother

Take your expectations off of me

Go ahead be hypocritical

It will only cause me to bend my knees

Therefore I will always be

What I was purposed and designed to be

You put no fear in me

Your opinions never mattered remotely close to what I see

My visions and dreams will never stop

Therefore you can't stop me physically

What doors you thought you closed

Was not for me

There was a door stopper

He's Mighty and oh so dope

Therefore I must keep moving

Regardless of what you thought was best for me

I've been planted & rooted in success

I've been watered to grow

Need I say anything more

Your Statistics do not define me.

Life added up quickly, this is where I refused to be what statistics expected I would be, I was lying in the hospital bed, made preparation to tie, clip, and burn my tubes, this was my third C-Section, I made up in my mind I will not go through this alone again, this is the last time, and life just kind of snowball and I was in the middle of it, I was constantly working two jobs, at a Childcare Facility, and a juvenile detention center with one day off, between these two jobs, had enough time in the day to prep my kids with dinner take them to my mother come back next morning take them to school until one day I fell asleep under the wheel. That particular morning on my way home I decided to wear my seat belt, the car flipped several times, falling into a ditch, I got out of the seat belt and walked out to the road for help, no bumps no bruises, after my car was towed, I was so driven I called a cab to take my kids to school and I still went right on to work, couple days later I had a crash and burn moment with God, I stopped for just a moment, I realized I was killing myself trying to prove myself and God took over from there and I just knew I had to take time and value what I have and be grateful, all I had was my babies, I slowed down, the income was not the same but I've learned it's not about how much you make, but what you do with what you make. When

I think I'm not doing a good job my babies remind me through their accomplishments and their words of encouragement to me sometimes, I'm proud and blessed beyond measure, my sons are awesome, my daughter is beautiful inside/out most of all they love and respect themselves and others.

CHAPTER 10

YOUR JOURNEY IS NOT OVER

Don't despise failure, it can be your best teacher, a guidance for the next step, and even there you may have more failure but it will be on a higher level, this time you will not fall so far back down, you will not find yourself starting from the very bottom again, there is more to you and you've grown more than your physical eyes can see, I want to use the theory of working out because to me it seems to be the toughest, what I learned in the process of working out, the results you see in the beginning is only water weight, disappointing right? Not at all, because there's progress and you've begun the process and you can't get to the fat until you release the water weight first, then there's breaking down bad fat and building muscle tissue, in my opinion, hurts the worst, because this is when you are really challenged to change your mindset then you can begin on the journey of building good fat, good muscle tissue, last but not least good healthy habits, and you have to fight to not fall back into the familiar, don't be afraid to keep moving forward, because eventually, you will cross that bridge, as I write these words, I think how I've fallen back into familiar ways out of fear and because it was easier to fall back than to go forward and see the change through, seeing my transformation, crossing that threshold when you began to enjoy your journey, you're to the point of no return.

Luke 12:48 When someone has been given much, much will be required in return; and when someone has been entrusted with much, even more will be required.

I wanted to use that scripture to make this point, once God has given and you've given yourself so much, there's no way you can settle for less, and much more will be required of you, it has become your routine, second nature, your expectations are greater, therefore your circle may change as well, meaning not everyone will continue the journey with you, everyone has a journey/path, don't get complacent in the change of direction, accept it for what it is, you can't change your direction predestine for you, I know we get scared sometimes and the fear of losing love ones along the way, I was not expecting my sister to leave here even though I knew she was very ill, I can say I wish she would have fought harder to stay, but I didn't know her pain, I can say she still had her kids to raise and she still had her goals to reach, but I didn't know where her journey began and end. I know there was more she wanted to do, she began her acting career and she was very successful in her career, her death was a reality check for me, proof that we don't know when and we don't know where, the reason we shouldn't waste time, our day will come because time does not rewind.

Last but not least I'm grateful for this opportunity and I'm grateful I was able to reach you, through my experiences thus far on this journey, there are two things I have not accomplished on this journey yet, but they are written because I believe and I know they will come to pass, no matter what may come my way, this book is just the beginning for me, I look forward to so much more, my faith is strong, and grace has no price.

1 John 4:19

We love because he first loved us.

Colossians 3:13

Bear with each other and forgive one another if any of you has a grievance against someone. Forgive as the Lord forgave you.

John 4:19

for without his love, love would cease to exist! Love your family and never forget where such an outpouring of love comes from.

1 Corinthians 13:4-7

Love is patient and kind; love does not envy or boast; it is not arrogant or rude. It does not insist on its own way; it is not irritable or resentful; it does not rejoice at wrongdoing, but rejoices with the truth. Love bears all things, believes all things, hopes all things, endures all things.

1 Corinthians 13:13

So now faith, hope, and love abide, these three; but the greatest of these is love.

Pat yourself on the back because you're on the path to an awesome adventure with your family, I love you but God loves you best. I truly believe Readers are Leaders.

CPSIA information can be obtained
at www.ICGtesting.com
Printed in the USA
BVHW072248141121
621672BV00005B/140